HONEST to GOD

*A Six-Step Prayer Challenge, Expanding
the Lord's Prayer with His Permission*

JED MOREHOUSE

ISBN 979-8-88832-457-8 (paperback)
ISBN 979-8-88832-459-2 (hardcover)
ISBN 979-8-88832-458-5 (digital)

Copyright © 2023 by Jed Morehouse

All rights reserved. No part of this publication may be reproduced, distributed, or transmitted in any form or by any means, including photocopying, recording, or other electronic or mechanical methods without the prior written permission of the publisher. For permission requests, solicit the publisher via the address below.

Christian Faith Publishing
832 Park Avenue
Meadville, PA 16335
www.christianfaithpublishing.com

Printed in the United States of America

ACKNOWLEDGMENT

First of all, I want to thank God for his love and patience with me. There are no accidents with God. What I call "failures" in my life, God calls a "process" and a "pathway of learning" how he works. His timing is perfect. I also want to thank my parents, James and Martha Morehouse, for taking me to church every Sunday and showing me the importance of serving God. I am blessed to have such loving parents that I can always turn to for love and support. I enjoy every moment of our time together. The eternal reward I and all of our family receive are because of your faithfulness to God. I want to thank my wife, Michelle, who has supported me through the whole process of writing this book. You have encouraged me and set my heart at ease many times. God certainly blessed me when he brought you in my life, and I don't say it enough. I want to thank my children: Shandra Morehouse, Natasha Dean, Morgan Edwards, and Miranda Edwards. I am blessed to have you in my life. You bring me love, joy, and laughter. I treasure all the times we spend together.

CHAPTER 1

The Beginning Word

Have you ever had someone try to change your way of thinking to match theirs? What's their motive? Why does it matter to them that you agree with them or their way of thinking? Obviously, they think they're right and you are wrong. A good example is politics. There are people on the left and people on the right. Each side has strong opinions, and most of the time, neither can be persuaded to follow the other side. Especially when they use phrases like, "You are wrong!" or yelling derogatory comments, rolling their eyes, or other disrespectful tactics. People, who use tactics like these, usually don't accomplish their goal of winning someone over to their way of thinking.

What would happen if both sides would sit down and discuss each other's sides in a civil matter? It still might not work, but you would give each side something to think about. It would also help if you were knowledgeable about the subject you are trying to persuade. If you have ever walked onto a car lot, you probably know about the pressure salesman. They will tell you the advantages of buying a car on their lot. The positives of buying that particular vehicle far outweigh the negatives. As a matter of fact, they would say the negatives are so minor, they aren't worth mentioning at all. They will also tell you that ten other people have looked at that vehicle today and are making a decision right now whether to buy this car or not. So you better hurry and sign the paperwork. If you wait and miss out on this vehicle, there will never be another deal like this again. I'm ashamed to say that in my early twenties, I would fall for that.

There are a lot of topics out there that causes debate. Some of those have to do with your location. For instance, if you live in Indiana, where I live, most of us love the game of basketball. However, the team you root for is cause for some heated discussions. Purdue University and Indiana University are about a hundred miles apart from each other, although they might as well be two different countries at war with each other. For example, Purdue is the United States, and IU is Iraq. Yes, I'm a Purdue fan. I may have just lost half my audience. My brother lives in Alabama. One of the first things he was asked when he arrived there was, "Are you for Alabama or Auburn?" How about people who live in Chicago: Cubs or White Sox? Other topics could be Pepsi versus Coke, McDonald's or Burger King, cats or dogs, and maybe one of the biggest one's as of recent years, Michael Jordan or LeBron James?

Here's a topic that has been debated for centuries: God versus science. I think most people would agree that it takes faith to believe in God. Science, on the other hand, deals with facts, right? I disagree. *Faith* is believing without seeing. Those of us who believe in God have never seen God in person. But at the same notion, the science community never witnessed the "big bang" or evolution taking place. Therefore, that belief is also by faith.

Either way, the start of this whole world and everything in it was caused by something supernatural. Whether molecules, three to four billion years ago, came together to form the Earth and every-thing in it or a supreme being, God, created everything—from land, seas, animals, and finally, human beings.

The first chapter is not intended to start arguments or judge-ment of anyone, but rather, ask the question: would you like to know if God is real?

You might ask why it's important to know how this whole world started or why it is important to know if God is real or not. If there is no God, then life really has no meaning. We live, we die, and that's it.

Those of us who believe in God have a hope of eternal life with God. Some of us have had a personal experience with God. I've gone to church ever since I can remember. So I was fortunate to get to know the stories in the Bible at an early age. I believed that God is the Creator of all things. A lot of people did not grow up attending church and may not know who God is and what he is all about. They may ask questions like, "How do you know God is real?" or "Why do you believe in God?" The simple answer is that I read the Bible and believe it to be true. The Bible will tell you everything that you need to know about God. We've all heard someone say, "But the Bible was written by man, human beings, just like us." This is true to a point, but those people were inspired by God. Think about it, if there is a God, and he knows all, and he's all powerful, and he is everywhere, don't you think he can inspire people to write books and put them in one big book called the Bible?

Christians are often referred to as freaks, Bible thumpers, and religious nuts. Feel free to put in the insults that you have heard. I think it's safe to say that most Christians feel sad that not everyone has had the experience with God that we have had and still have. We try to share our beliefs with people who don't believe. There are different ways of expressing or sharing our position that we call salvation. Some people engage in street-preaching. I, personally, have not seen that as an effective way of sharing the faith. They would usually get ridiculed and made fun of. Some people engage in strong debates. Other people, afraid of rejection, just sit in church every Sunday and leave the rest of the world alone because we don't want to ruffle any feathers or be called judgmental. I think for most of my life I would put myself in the last category. By the way, not all Christians are judgmental. Some of us try to love everyone and share our faith in love just as Jesus did.

Oh! This is the first time I mentioned that name (Jesus), isn't it? Yes, Jesus is the most important part of Christianity. Jesus is the son of God whom he sent down to earth to save us from our sins by dying on the cross as a sacrifice so that we may inherit eternal life. You know the Easter story.

Think about that name for a moment—Jesus. It's the most powerful name in history that makes everybody cringe. Yes, everybody! You don't believe me? Think about people who don't go to church or believe in God. If someone was to come up to them at a party, or even in private, and ask them, "Do you know Jesus as your savior?" They would either get angry with you or say things like, "I don't want to hear your preaching." Or, at the very least, get real uncomfortable (cringe). If that same unbeliever is talking to the same believer and says the exact same name, but in a different context, it would have the opposite effect for each person. For instance, he says, "Jesus Christ, where are you going now?" Using Jesus's name in that way makes Christians uncomfortable (cringe). We call that taking the Lord's name in vain. Worse than any four-letter word people use. What other name in history has that much power?

An important part of knowing and believing in God is, like I said earlier, reading the Bible. Another important thing we do as Christians is communicate with God, and we do that through prayer or talking with God.

Everybody knows about prayer. Many people ask for prayers. Some people who ask for prayers don't even go to church or believe in God. So I wonder whom they're praying to. When people are desperate and can't control a situation, they will pray and ask people to pray for them. Especially on Facebook, you'll get a lot of, "I'll be praying" or the praying hands emoji. I wonder how many people actually pray when they tell someone that they will be praying. When they do pray, are they expecting an answer from God? If the situation has a positive outcome, I wonder how many people give God the credit.

I've heard people say, "What good is praying going to do? God won't answer." Or they don't think God would care about them. They surely wouldn't pray for everyday things in their life. I must admit that I had those doubts at times about praying for everyday things in my life as well. But as I started reading the Bible more and understanding what it says, I changed my way of thinking. In John 15:7 (NIV), Jesus is speaking,

> If you remain in me and my words remain in
> you, ask whatever you wish, and it will be done
> for you.

Now, if that's the only thing you read in the Bible, and you say, "Cool, I'm going to ask for a million dollars," you might get disillusioned about the Bible. That's why you have to read the whole Bible to find out what God's character is. If you read another book and verse in the bible such as James 4:3–4 (NIV), it states,

> When you ask, you do not receive because you ask with wrong motives, that you may spend what you get on your pleasures.

In 1 John 5:14–15 (NIV):

> This is the confidence we have in approaching God: That if we ask anything according to his will, he hears us. If we know that he hears us-whatever we ask—we know that we have what we ask of him.

So what is God's will for our life? I believe John 3: 16–17 (NIV) sums it up pretty well.

> For God so loved the world that he gave his one and only son, that whoever believes in him shall not perish but have eternal life. For God did not send his son into the world to condemn the world, but to save the world through him.

There are two things I believe everyone wants to know: the truth and peace of mind. How do we achieve those two things? With everything we have to face in this world, it can be hard to find peace of mind. Many people have anxiety over several different things like living in a difficult marriage, PTSD, raising children, work and supporting a family on a low budget, health issues, and many more. It may seem like they are never-ending; finding peace can be challenging, but I have found a peace that comes from trusting in the Lord. But I don't expect you to take my word as "truth." Instead, I would like to challenge you to find the peace that I have by going right to the source—God himself. Go to a place where you are alone and there are no distractions and start praying to God. You can say this simple prayer: "God, if you are real, show me." Short, sweet, and honest. I believe when we are honest with God, he respects that. Whenever I am honest and humble before God, he always answers my prayers. Does he answer right away? Not always. Sometimes I pray the same prayer over and over. That shows that I am serious about wanting an answer.

So I challenge you. If you're not sure if God is real, ask him. It takes about five seconds. Ask him every day. What have you got to lose? More importantly, what have you got to gain? Psalm 34:8 (NIV) says, "Taste and see that the Lord is good: blessed is the one who takes refuge in Him."

Have you ever looked at some food that had been prepared and a friend says to you, "That dish is really good." But yet another one of your friends says, "That's really not that good." Who do you believe? Both of them are your friend, and you don't believe either one would lie to you. It all comes down to personal taste. So in order to find out if you like it, you're going to have to taste it for yourself and not take anyone's word for it. That's what I'm asking you to do. This is between you and God. Be honest with God. Tell him what you're thinking. Tell him your doubts. He already knows what you're thinking and your doubts. If you open your heart and mind, some kind of blessing will follow. In 2 Peter 3:9 (NIV), it says,

> The Lord is not slow in keeping his promise as some understand slowness. Instead, He is patient with you, not wanting any one to perish, but everyone to come to repentance.

Prayer Challenge Number 1:

God if you're real, show me, and speak to my heart.

Taste and see that the Lord is good, blessed
is the one who takes refuge in Him.

—Psalm 34:8 (NIV)

God if you're real, show me, and speak to my heart.

CHAPTER 2

Satisfy My Hunger

Have you ever set life goals for yourself? I think it's safe to say that most of us have some sort of plan for our lives. Whether it's a small plan or a big plan, there's always a goal that we want to accomplish. Some people go to college and become doctors, lawyers, engineers, health-care workers or businessmen or women. Other people want to make money right away, so they enter the workforce, maybe in manufacturing, food service, or retail.

I believe God places us in certain jobs for a reason. I spent twenty years in a factory. I got hired twelve days before my twentieth birthday. At that time, I was happy to get a career job. I did a lot of growing up there. I also found out quickly that people who were ten to twenty years older than me did not act like the adults I was used to being around. Like I said earlier, my parents took my siblings and me to church every Sunday. We didn't miss church unless there was a snow emergency. I knew most of the stories in the Bible starting with Adam and Eve in Genesis to Revelation where we get a glimpse of the future events that take place before the Lord comes back and takes believers to heaven to live with God forever. So most of the adults I had contact with were from the church. They were respectful, they didn't lie about me or harass me or curse me out just because they could. I was pretty naive about the world outside of my circle.

It didn't take them long to find out that I was a Christian. I didn't swear, I didn't smoke, drink, or engage in immoral activities. I felt alone and out of place most of the time. I felt persecuted because of my belief and how I chose to live my life.

Life is all about choices. The choices we make define who we are and what we believe. Our thoughts and beliefs shape our lives. If you were to ask someone what is on their mind everyday or what thought controls their mind or motivates them on daily basis, you would probably get a few different answers. One might say, "Money, so I can provide for my family and enjoy the things I want." Others might say, "Time off of work, so I can spend more time with my family and friends." No matter what motivates you or controls your thoughts, I think we can all agree that having peace and happiness is the key to living a fulfilled life.

As a Christian, following God's commandments and his will for our lives should be a priority. God's commandments were given to Moses. We all know or should know the Ten Commandments. Although, I'll be honest, I don't hear too much preaching or a lot of time spent on these Commandments. You can find these in the book of Exodus 20:1–17 (NIV). So here they are:

1. You shall have no other gods before me. (put God first)
2. You shall not make idols. (worship God only)
3. You shall not take the name of the Lord God in vain. (use God's name with respect)
4. Remember the Sabbath day and keep it holy. (self-explanatory)
5. Honor your mother and father. (respect your parents)
6. You shall not murder. (self-explanatory)
7. You shall not commit adultery. (be faithful in marriage)
8. You shall not steal. (self-explanatory)
9. You shall not bear false witness against your neighbor. (don't lie)
10. You shall not covet. (don't want what others have)

Our world is in trouble, agree?

There are several scriptures in the Bible that explains the will of God in our lives.

"For I know the plans I have for you," declares the Lord. "Plans to prosper you and not harm you, Plans to give you hope and a future." (Jeremiah 29:11 NIV)

Then he, (Jesus) said to them all, "Whoever wants to be my disciple must deny himself and take up their cross daily and follow me." (Luke 9:23 NIV)

In other words, live like Jesus did, sharing the good news about the Lord. Now, does God expect us to do everything the same way another person does it? No, God has a specific plan for each of us. So how do we know what God's plan is for us? The answer awaits you in the word of God. Psalm 119:105 (NIV) says, "Your word is a lamp unto my feet and light unto my path."

Prayer is also important. How important is prayer? Read any of the gospels: Matthew, Mark, Luke, or John. Before Jesus did anything, he went off by himself to pray to God the Father.

There are two parts of prayer. Talking to God and listening to God. When talking to God, we need to ask him for strength, wisdom, and courage for what we are going to face in our daily life. We don't know what the day will bring. But God does, and he will walk us through situations or trials when they arise.

Listening to God is one of the hardest things to describe to someone. If God doesn't speak to us in an audible voice, how do we know God is speaking to us? In my experience, God will place something in my mind and I'll know it's from God, because my mind wouldn't have gone there on my own, if that makes sense. When God gives you an answer to prayer and you know in your heart that it was from God, the joy that you feel in that moment is indescribable.

A lot of people only pray when they have an urgent need. I don't know about you, but I would always feel guilty about praying for a need if I haven't prayed in a while. God does answer prayers, but he desires a relationship with us all the time, not just when a need arises. If we, as Christians, are supposed to pattern our lives after Jesus, we have to serve others and spend time with God. What would happen if we talked to our spouse only on occasions? That wouldn't be considered a good marriage. My wife and I talk everyday and share everything. Sometimes, we can't wait to tell each other about what happened that day. If we can't talk in person, we call each other on the phone. That's what God desires. He wants us to want to talk to him. He wants us to be excited about spending time with him.

Here's the crazy part: even as Christians, we know we need to spend time in God's Word and pray to him. But oftentimes, we struggle to make time for him. We work eight to twelve hours a day, have chores to do when we get home—supper to fix, kids to chase, younger children to bathe. When do we have time for God? I struggled with that for years. I would go to church on Sunday, hear the message, and get convicted. Then I would tell God, "I'm going to do it this time, God. I'm going to read your Word and pray every day. I would for about a day or two, maybe a week, and then I would fall back into being too busy again.

What does the devil hate the most? People praying! He will do everything he can to distract you. He will tell you that you are too busy to pray.

Could it be that he knows how powerful prayer is? Let's not be deceived. The devil, Satan, is powerful. He can place temptations or distractions right in front of you and make you think, *It will be okay, it doesn't matter. Besides, no one will ever know.* He is a liar!

God is more powerful, and Satan knows it. So we need to put our defenses up against the devil to defeat him like it says in Ephesians 6:10–18 (NIV) (the armor of God, which we will go into detail in a later chapter).

So how do we become consistent in our prayer life? Remember when I said, "I'm going to do it this time, God?" Then a few days later, I would go back to my old ways? The problem is that I said "I" a lot. Finally, "I" realized that I can't do it by my own power. I can't tell you how many diets I've tried in my lifetime. I would get frustrated with a diet really quick. I didn't have patience. I didn't think any diet worked. Then after a hip replacement, I swallowed my pride and said, "I can't do this on my own." So I made an appointment with a doctor who specializes in weight loss. I ended up losing forty pounds in about four months.

I did the same thing with my prayer life. I got honest with God and prayed a simple prayer: "Lord, reveal yourself to me and give me a hunger for you and your Word." I repeated that prayer every day. What I was basically telling God was that I didn't have a hunger for him or his Word but wanted to. Is that pretty gutsy to admit that to God? Not really. He already knew that. He was just waiting for me to admit that to myself. I believe that he honored my honesty. He wants us to depend on him. That's why he desires our prayers. He wants us to realize our need of him. Before I knew it, God was opening up his Word to me and giving me insight that I never had before. Now I can't get enough. I pray every day. I even have a chair in my living room that I call my "prayer chair." I meet God there approximately two hours every morning. I set my alarm early in the morning when no one else is up and start my day off with a blessing. Ironically, that's the same place that my mother used to sit and do her bible study and prayer time. So God is familiar with that area in my home.

I talk to God about everything, just like I would with my wife, family, and friends. Since I've been spending time with God every day, I feel he speaks to me more frequently. He has opened doors and has given me guidance more often. All because I was honest, and I humbled myself before him. As in Philippians 4:13 (NIV),

> I can do all things through Christ who strengthens me.

Prayer Challenge Number 2:

> *Lord, reveal yourself to me, and give me a hunger for you and your Word.*

> Taste and see that the Lord is good, blessed
> is the one who takes refuge in Him.

> —Psalm 34:8 (NIV)

CHAPTER 3

A Light unto My Path

After asking God to reveal himself to you and give you a hunger for him and his Word, you'll be in a new era in your life. You'll be in God's Word more. You'll be praying more. And if you're like me, that hunger will turn into passion. This is an exciting time. Just like meeting your future spouse. Remember when dating and you couldn't wait to see him or her? The anticipation of getting to spend time with that new love in your life, which makes your whole body feel warm inside? That's the way I felt when God gave me the hunger that I asked him.

When I started spending time with God every day, he started placing things in my heart. He was leading me in directions that I never thought of by myself.

God has a plan for every one of his followers. Whether we follow those plans or promptings, are up to us. Those plans are to further his kingdom. Proverbs 3:5–6 (NIV) says,

> Trust in the Lord with all of your heart and lean
> not on your own understanding; in all your ways
> submit to Him, and He will make your paths
> straight.

Remember, God doesn't need us to fulfill his ultimate plan, but he gives us an opportunity to be blessed if we follow his plans for us.

You may find out that the plan he has for you is something you never thought you would or could do.

Consider Abraham. He was called "a friend of God." What must we do to be called "a friend of God"? Love God with all your heart. Trust God with all your heart. We can accomplish this by spending time talking with him, asking for guidance, and obeying God when he gives you guidance, just like Abraham did. Genesis 12:1–3 (NIV) says,

> The Lord had said to Abram, "Go from your country, your people and your father's household to a land I will show you. I will make you into a great nation, And I will bless you, I will make your name great and you will be a blessing. I will bless those who bless you, and whoever curses you I will curse, and all the peoples on earth will be blessed through you.

That was a promise God gave to Abraham. We as Christians know about "Father Abraham." God gave Abraham and his wife, Sarah, a son when Abraham was a hundred years old and when Sarah was ninety years old. Think about that for a moment. Most people, if they make it to a hundred years of age, would have children who would be in their seventies or eighties. Their grandchildren would be in their fifties or sixties. Their great-grandchildren would be in their twenties and thirties. You get the idea. So the first miracle was giving them a child at their age. The second miracle was giving Abraham and Sarah patience and stamina to raise a child at that age. Abraham didn't live long enough to witness the birth of the nation of Israel, which was named after Abraham's grandson, Jacob. (God changed Jacob's name to Israel.) Abraham made an impact on a whole nation and literally every nation because he was faithful and trusting to God. If we are faithful and trusting to God, he can also do great things in us. Once we start focusing on God, reading his Word, and praying for his will to be done, he will lead you in a different and exciting new direction in your life. Does this mean you won't have any more problems in your life? No. But if you are faithful to God and you trust him, he will see you through those tough times and give you a great testimony. Afterward, you will see those trying times as a blessing from God.

There are lessons to be learned from the trials in our lives. Every character in the Bible that God used faced trials at some point in their life. Joseph, who was the great-grandson of Abraham, got sold into slavery by his brothers. He accepted his fate, trusted in God, and became a man of respect in Egypt—a foreign land that he started out as a slave.

Moses, born a Hebrew from the line of Israel, was raised in Pharaoh's house as an Egyptian. After he found out he was actually an Israelite, he ended up fleeing from Egypt after killing an Egyptian to escape the wrath of Pharaoh. Later, God spoke to Moses and told him to go back to Egypt and lead the Israelites out of Egypt where they were slaves. Moses was an unlikely candidate for that task because he couldn't speak well. He also felt unworthy for that huge task. But Moses believed God and had faith in God, so he accepted that huge honor. Moses did lead the people out of Israel with many miracles along the way. God didn't show Moses a step-by-step plan. God provided a way even when their backs were against the wall.

God uses ordinary people to do extraordinary things. Peter was an uneducated fisherman when Jesus called him to follow him. Jesus taught him, blessed him, and anointed him, and God used Peter after Jesus's death and resurrection in a mighty way. After Jesus ascended to heaven, he sent the Holy Spirit down to fill the disciples and other followers. That way, the Lord would be speaking to their hearts. They didn't need the Holy Spirit when Jesus was on the earth because they had Jesus in person. He *was* the Holy Spirit in person. After receiving the Holy Spirit, Peter preached for the first time where three thousand people were cut to the heart and converted that day. Considering how many times Peter put his foot in his mouth and the fact that, just a short time ago, he denied even knowing Jesus, that was pretty amazing. But since Peter had been in constant fellowship with Jesus and praying continually, God used him in an extraordinary way.

Hebrews 13:8 (NIV) says, "Jesus Christ is the same yesterday, today, and forever." Therefore he is the same God who promised

Abraham a nation, the same God who was with Moses and parted the seas, the same God who filled Peter with the Holy Spirit so he could preach a sermon that converted three thousand souls to Christ, and the same God who can do great things through us if we decide to devote ourselves to God's Word and prayer.

Another story that everybody knows in the Bible is the story of David and Goliath. Goliath was a giant from the Philistines, a strong man, whom no one in Israel wanted to go fight against alone. But David, who was just a boy, decided to fight the giant because he was disrespecting the God of Israel that David served and loved. David was a lot smaller than Goliath, and I imagine everyone at the battle lines thought that this would be the end of David. But David's faith in God was so strong that he went out confident that God was on his side. David *did* kill Goliath with sling and a stone, but those were not David's biggest weapons.

In 1 Samuel 17:45 (NIV), David said to the Philistine, "You come against me with a sword, spear, and a javelin, but I come against you in the name of the Lord almighty, the God of the armies of Israel, whom you have defiled." David didn't even mention his sling. He gave all the credit to God. David's faith in God is what won the battle. "Faith is confident in what we hope for and assurance about what we don't see" (Hebrews11:1 NIV).

Are there giants in your life that seem impossible to conquer? Are there situations that you don't have a good answer for? Sometimes we all feel helpless at one time or another. Isaiah 55:8–9 (NIV) says,

> "For my thoughts are not your thoughts, neither
> are your ways, my ways," declares the Lord. "As
> heavens are higher than the earth, so are my ways
> higher than your ways and my thoughts higher
> than your thoughts."

When we don't see an answer, God has the answer. So why don't we swallow our pride and let God take control of our problems? That's the problem, isn't it? We like to be in control or we like people to think we are in control. When we devote ourselves to studying his word and prayer, God will change the direction of our lives. Some people think that's pretty scary especially if that involves a major change like quitting a job. I promise you, if it's God's will for you to quit your job, he has a bigger blessing awaiting you. God may not want you to quit your job. He places people in certain jobs for a reason. Maybe your coworkers need someone like you because you may be the only person they know that represents God. I've heard someone say that they were afraid to pray for God's will for their life because he might send them to Africa. I'm pretty sure if God wants you to go to Africa, he will put that desire in your heart.

Changing direction in your life, maybe just changing the way you think, or changing your habits or the way you handle adversity in your life—God may lead you in an area that you think is impossible for you. God specializes in the impossible. He gave Abraham and Sarah a son in their old age. He instructed Noah to build the biggest boat in history (at that time, with primitive tools). He led Moses and his people though the sea that he parted. He told Joshua and the Israelites to march around Jericho for six days, seven times on the seventh day, blowing trumpets, so that the walls of Jericho fell down. David killed Goliath. Peter walked on water. All these characters had one thing in common: they believed and trusted in God. God saw qualities in each one of these men that they didn't see in themselves. How much do you believe and trust God? How much time do you devote to God? God might just show you a quality in you that you don't know you have.

The third prayer challenge I want to encourage you to try is to pray this prayer:

Lord, lead me and change my direction, if necessary, so I can serve you the way you want me to.

Taste and see that the Lord is good, blessed
is the one who takes refuge in him.

—Psalm 34:8 (NIV)

CHAPTER 4

Conquering Temptation

What is the hardest part of being a Christian? I think most of us would agree that it's the feeling of not living up to the Christian standards (God's standards); it takes self-discipline and a lot of it. Consider an Olympic athlete. They have to have self-discipline in order to win the ultimate prize: the gold medal. They train for several years, not just one or two years. Some of these athletes start training as young as eight or nine years old. How does a young boy or girl get that kind of discipline to be able to endure that much training? How do they keep from getting frustrated along the way? Each athlete has their own coach. The coach teaches them how to compete; they teach them proper techniques. They encourage them and tell them that they have the potential to be great. They won't let them compete until they are ready. However, they may allow them to fail a few times so they won't get complacent. If that happens, they take a step back and work a little harder to get better.

In my junior high school, there was a sign on the wall that said, "The difference between good and great is a little extra effort." Even after all the training, the young man, woman, boy, or girl goes through, there will still be a time when they have a doubt in their mind that says, "I can't do this, it's too hard." They might think about quitting several times during their training. Some may quit. Others fight through those thoughts and keep on working through those difficult times. That's called self-discipline. When it's time to compete in the big event, they are ready to face the competition with confidence. But even after all that training, they will still be nervous, afraid of making one mistake that might cost them the prize. That's why in every event, if you look at the sidelines, you will always see their coach in their corner, still encouraging them, still teaching them, still supporting and comforting them.

As a Christian, we also need training and self-discipline to live our lives that's pleasing to God. The Christian life is not easy, but it's still the best way to live. It will be a lifelong process to live as Christ wants us to live. At the same time, living a Christlike life will give us peace, joy, and contentment. We were born in a sinful world. We have to battle things such as selfishness, greed, jealousy, anger, resentment, unforgiveness, and self-control. Just like the Olympic athlete, we are in a race that we want to win. This is a marathon race so it's going to take a lot of patience.

> Do you not know that in a race, all runners run, but only one gets the prize? Run in such a way to get the prize. Everyone who competes in the games go into strict training. They do it to get a crown that will not last, but we do it as to get a crown that last will last forever. (1 Corinthians 9:24–25 NIV)

Temptation is nothing new. The first temptation was in the Garden of Eden when the devil, Satan, appeared to Eve as a serpent and deceived her into disobeying God's command to not eat the fruit of the tree of knowledge of good and evil. After she took a bite, she gave it to Adam to eat so she wouldn't be in trouble alone. But let's not be too hard on Eve. She was just having a rebellious childhood that she never had a chance to experience, because well, she was never a child. Besides, if Adam or Eve never sinned, Cain, their son, would have probably been the first sinner.

All throughout the Bible, there are people who fall into temptation. Some of those really loved God with all their heart. Take David, the king of Israel, a man after God's own heart. God was with him when he killed a lion and a bear while they were attacking his sheep that he was attending. He slayed the giant named Goliath when he was a young man when no one in the army was brave enough to fight the giant. After David was king, God was still with him. He would lead the army in wars against other kingdoms and come out victorious. But even the strong and very faithful servants of God can be tempted and fall. One time David sent the army out to fight in a war. But David stayed behind this time. He was wondering around on his balcony, probably feeling lonely, when his eyes caught a woman bathing herself. David was mesmerized by her beauty, and he sent for her and had an affair with her. He thought he could have an affair, send her back, and that would be the end. No one would ever have to know. But she got pregnant with David's baby. Long story short, David had her husband killed by sending him to the front line of the battle where the battle was fierce. That way, everyone would think that she got pregnant with David's baby after her husband died, but sin is never unpunished. Even if you ask forgiveness, there are still consequences. In that situation, I heard a saying that goes, "You have to keep your eyes on the Creator and not on his creation."

We will always get in trouble when we think we can handle temptation on our own. How many times have you heard of a minister or priest fall into temptation? It's sad and humiliating for everyone involved. Non-Christians have a heyday with these situations. No one, including Christians, is perfect. Romans 3:23–24 (NIV) says, "For all have sinned and fall short of the glory of God and are justified freely by his grace through the redemption that came by Jesus Christ."

Just like the athletes, we also have a coach in our corner. Sometimes, we have to call timeout and go talk to him. A good time to talk to him is when being tempted. Asking Jesus, our coach, to help us fight those desires and deliver us from temptation is always a great idea. Remember, it's not a sin to be tempted. It's what happens after you get tempted that counts. When temptation comes, there will be that voice in your head that says, "Go ahead! No one will ever know. What's it going to hurt?" That voice comes from Satan himself. He will try to do anything to get you to fail in your Christian walk. The Lord isn't up on his throne waiting for us to fail. He wants us to succeed in life. We are created so we could fellowship with God. He desires us to have a peaceful life. He is on our side and wants the best for us.

> If God is for us, who can be against us? He who did not spare his own son, but gave him up for all of us. How will he not also, along with him graciously give us all things? (Romans 8:31–32 NIV)

The key to having the strength of Christ is not only asking him for strength when temptation is right in front of you but asking for strength before temptation comes. Had David done that, he wouldn't have been in that situation that his eyes caught him off guard.

> I can do all things through Christ who strengthens me. (Philippians 4:13 NKJV)

Your salvation isn't lost because you sinned. You are still saved by grace. Sin may come at a cost and most of the time with regret. Those of us who love God have to realize that Satan will work extra hard on us because we are a threat to him and what he wants to accomplish.

> Consider it pure joy, my brothers and sisters, whenever you face trials of many kinds, because you know that the testing of your faith produces perseverance. Let perseverance finish its work so that you may be mature and complete, not lacking in anything. (James 1:2–4 NIV)

We may fall into a certain sin several times before we are able to conquer it.

When a toddler is learning to walk, how many times do they fall down? Several times, right? As parents, what do we say? "Well, you tried, you're just never going to walk," and give up on them? Of course not. We help them back to their feet, wipe their tears, and encourage them to try again, and again, and again. We don't give up on our children because we know that eventually they'll be walking. We are very patient with them, and when they succeed, we make a big deal about it. We put it on video, share it with our family and friends, and post it on Facebook for the world to see. When we fall into temptation and fail time and time again, God is right there to pick us up, wipe our tears, and say, "Try again. This time, *focus on me!*" Before we know it, we will be taking long strides with confidence. These are called spiritual battles which we will face most of our lives, and if God is by our side, he will give us the strength to win those battles.

Once we have become a child of God, it's time to start training for battle. Yes, battle. Life is a battlefield full of mines and traps. So how do we train for this battle? Before we had fighter jets, ships, assault weapons, and long-range missiles, there was hand-to-hand combat. In the early ages, they had armor: helmets, body armor, shields, swords, etc. In the battle that Christians face, we have what we call the armor of God found in Ephesians 6:13–17 (NIV). The Apostle Paul wrote down six items of the armor of God, but do we understand what each of them mean? Let's go through them.

We have the "Belt of Truth." A soldier's belt holds and fastens weapons that are used against the enemy. The belt is around the waist close to the body with easy access. The Bible is the weapon against our enemy therefore we need to keep it close.

The "Breastplate of Righteousness." The breastplate covers the vital organs: the heart, lungs, kidneys, and liver. If a soldier didn't wear this breastplate and got attacked or pierced in this area, it would most likely result in death. Righteousness means "acting in accordance with divine law, free from guilt and sin." We must be knowledgeable in God's Word, which will allow us to understand and know how to live a righteous life.

"The Feet fitted with the readiness that comes from the gospel of peace." A soldier doesn't go into battle without shoes. A good pair of shoes (or boots) will help you walk through rough areas without pain or stumbling. With these shoes Paul talks about, we will be ready to walk boldly in the gospel (good news) of peace, sharing the good news about Christ.

"The Shield of Faith." Having faith in Christ will influence the way we live. Just like a shield would deflect the weapons of the enemy, God's Word and the promise we receive from him, will protect us from the weapons of our enemy, Satan.

"The Helmet of Salvation." The helmet protects the mind. The soldier puts it on when going head-to-head with the enemy. Satan attacks us with lies and tries to get into our head. With the helmet of salvation protecting our minds, we can detect all the lies that Satan tries to pollute us with. Salvation comes from the Lord. Therefore, the Lord is our protection.

"The Sword of the Spirit." The sword represents the Word of God. Just like a sword can pierce the heart physically, the Sword of the Spirit (the Word of God) can also pierce the heart in a spiritual way. The Word of God is an effective weapon that we can use against the devil. But to use the sword effectively, we have to have lots of training. We can't be handed a sword and go right into battle. At the same notion, we can't be handed a Bible and go out preaching to our friends the next day. We have to read and ask the Holy Spirit for understanding and guidance.

> All scripture is God-breathed and useful for teaching, rebuking, correcting, and training in righteousness. (2 Timothy 3:16–17 NIV)

If our beliefs are not rooted in God's Word, we can't expect to fight battles for Christ. Everyone has to deal with temptation in their life. Even Jesus, at the beginning of his ministry, was tempted by the devil. Jesus, of course, prevailed against him. Satan knows what temptation each person struggles with. Resisting temptation is hard, and we can't be that arrogant to think we can handle that on our own. When Jesus was teaching his disciples how to pray, he included that in his model prayer: "Lead us not into temptation and deliver us from evil." Jesus is telling us that we can't resist temptation on our own. We need our heavenly Father's help.

The Fourth Prayer Challenge is:

Lord, help me to fight temptation and deliver me from evil. Help me to put on the full armor of God as instructed in Ephesians.

Taste and see that the Lord is good, blessed
is the one who takes refuge in Him.

—Psalm 34:8 (NIV)

CHAPTER 5

Forgive and Be Forgiven

Now that we have asked God to help us fight temptation, does that mean we will live a sinless life from now on? Unfortunately, no, although it's certainly the goal, but the fact is, we all have a human nature. The tempter is always looking for ways to tempt us. For example, money is a big temptation. Working on Sundays pays more in most jobs. Although sometimes, working on Sundays is unavoidable. Hospitals are a good example. Everyone is thankful that there are people working in hospitals on Sundays. But the temptation to work every Sunday for the higher pay keeps us away from spending time with God and other believers, which is important for us to fellowship with like-minded people. If we don't have a consistent time that we set apart to spend with God, we often find ourselves falling away from God. We may not notice it at first, but one day, we find ourselves distant from God and we don't know how it happened. That's the way the devil works. After falling away from God, if you're like me, you start having guilty feelings. What do we do now? We must ask God for forgiveness, which means humbling ourselves before God.

I remember when I was a child and I took something away from my sibling. When my father or mother found out, they would make me apologize even when I didn't feel like it. When I was younger, I found it hard to say "I'm sorry." I have no idea why. I guess it was that humbling feeling that I didn't like or the fact that I had to humble myself in front of my brothers. When I became an adult, I feel like I apologize all the time. I walk around the corner at the same time another person is taking the same corner in the opposite direction. We don't run into each other as we meet, but we both take a stutter step out of each other's way and both of us would say, "*Oops*, sorry," and keep walking our own direction. Another time, I walked up to vending machine to get a pop, and there was someone ahead of me. After they got their drink, they turned around to me and say sorry. This meant, "Sorry for taking so long." If I can't wait ten seconds at a vending machine, I have serious problems.

On the other hand, there are situations that would compel us to ask forgiveness from someone. Have you ever said a mean thing to someone in a stressful moment or yelled at someone out of frustration? Do you remember how you felt afterward? I'm a pretty sensitive person, and I try to be patient with everyone. But sometimes I slip and show my frustration, and I would say something that is taken in a hurtful way whether I meant it that way or not. When I do that, I don't get a whole lot of sleep until I ask forgiveness from that person. I was taught at a young age the golden rule: "Do to others what you would have them do to you."

Along with the golden rule, my parents had a set of rules that we had to abide by: don't swear, do chores that are asked of you, be home by the time set by them according, to our age at the time, and respect them and other adult authority. If any of these rules were broken, we were made to say we're sorry. But there were still consequences for breaking these rules or being disobedient. Punishments are necessary in life so we can learn. If a child throws a fit and the parent gives in to their tantrums, they are doing their child an injustice because what they learn is that if they act out, they will get what they want. When that child gets older and act the same way, the world will not be a pushover like Mom and Dad. No one wants an employee that acts that way.

God has rules as well, and in our house, those rules were just as important, if not more important than my parents' rules. When breaking God's rules, we are to ask God for forgiveness. In 1 John 1:9 (NKJV), it says, "If we confess our sins, he is faithful and just to forgive us our sins and to cleanse us from all unrighteousness." Likewise, every job has rules that need to be followed. If an employee fails to follow a rule, they will get called out for their mistake. Then that employee would have one of two choices to make. They can continue to ignore the rule, which would probably get them fired, or they can apologize for the mistake and say they will do better next time. The employer will usually accept their apology and allow them to keep their job, mostly because of their attitude and remorse.

The same goes for God. If we keep doing things against God's commandments without remorse, he will not forgive us. But if we confess that what we did was wrong and vow to ourselves and God that we will not do it again, or try to not do it again, God will forgive us.

There are sixty-six books in the Bible. All throughout the Bible, we read about men and women of God and their faith and trust in God. We read about the victories that are won with God's help. But every righteous person mentioned in the Bible also sinned against God at some point in their life and had to ask for forgiveness.

Have you ever thought of a person that was so wicked that they were beyond forgiveness? I think we all know of people that we think deserves no mercy. If we are honest, we can think of people that are unforgivable and on their way to hell for sure.

In February 2017, close to my hometown, two girls were murdered. As of 2022, the murders have not been solved. This case changed the community and placed them on the national map. If this person is ever caught, he will receive little or no forgiveness by most of the people in this small town or the world, probably. Can God forgive this person? In the book of 2 Chronicles chapter 33, there was a man named Manasseh. He became the fourteenth king of Israel at the age of twelve. He reigned in Israel for fifty-five years. This story caught my attention because of how evil this person was. First, he worshipped other gods instead of the one true God. He built an altar, to those pagan gods in a place where the Lord said, "My name will remain in Jerusalem forever." Manasseh sacrificed his own sons in fire. He practiced sorcery, witchcraft, and consulted with mediums and psychics. Even after God spoke to Manasseh and his people, they ignored his warnings. So God sent the Assyrian's army, and they took Manasseh as a prisoner and bound him in chains.

> But while in deep distress, Manasseh sought the Lord God and sincerely humbled himself before the God of his ancestors. And when he prayed, the Lord listened to him and was moved by his request. So the Lord brought Manasseh back to Jerusalem and to his kingdom. Then Manasseh finally realized that the Lord alone is God! (2 Chronicles 33:12–13 NLT)

In the world we live in, Manasseh would have been treated like Charles Manson or Jeffrey Dahmer, going down in history as one of the worst and notorious people that ever lived. But God is the only one who truly knows the heart of a person and if they are truly remorseful. After reading this story in the Bible and how God's anger can be reversed by simply asking for forgiveness and turning from that way of life, I realized that God can and will forgive anyone who desires to change. The best thing that can happen to people who steal and murder is to get caught. People, who may get away with those things in this life and don't repent and ask God to forgive them, will not escape the eternal judgment from God.

The second part of forgiveness is that we must forgive others who sin against us. In Matthew 6:12 (NLT), it says, "and forgive us our sins, as we have forgiven those who sin against us." That's a part of the Lord's Prayer that he gave for us. Jesus never had to say that part of the prayer for himself because he was perfect and never sinned. All the other parts of the prayer, I believe he prayed to God the Father in his personal time with God. After Jesus gave us that prayer, he backtracks to focus on forgiveness as a point of emphasis. Verse 14 of Matthew chapter 6 says, "If you forgive those who sin against you, your Father in heaven will forgive you. But if you refuse to forgive others, your Father will not forgive your sins."

I think it's safe to say that we all have had someone wrong us in some way in our lifetime. Sometimes, we can forgive them fairly easy.

But there are times when we get hurt so bad that we have a hard time forgiving them or letting go of that memory. At this point, I would usually write down an example of a hurt that someone has caused me, but that would be bringing up old wounds that I have already forgiven. Also, I don't want to point anyone out. That would be hurtful to them and that would not please God or make me feel good. Sometimes I wish that when we forgive, we forget, but forgetting is not possible for us to do and maybe for good reason. I believe that every bad experience we have is a lesson from God. We just might not see it for a while.

Jesus grants forgiveness to all believers who ask for forgiveness, although we don't deserve it and we can't earn it. Therefore, if we are to live as Christ did, we are to forgive others in the same way. Unforgiveness is emotional bondage that consumes our minds with hatred and thoughts of revenge. Jesus gave a great example of forgiveness while he was on the cross. Speaking to God of those who were responsible for crucifying him, he said in Luke 23:34 (NIV) "Father forgive them for they don't know what they are doing." He said that in the midst of the pain, anguish, and rejection of that moment. He could have called ten thousand angels to rescue him and that would have shown everyone there that he was who he said he was. But thankfully, he went through death for our sake. Giving his life as a sacrifice, he paid for all of our sins, past and future.

Peter once asked Jesus in Matthew 18:21–22 (NIV), he said, "'Lord, how many times should I forgive my brother or sister who sins against me? Up to seven times?' Jesus answers, 'I tell you, not seven times but seventy times seven.'" Some of you might have thought what I was thinking the first time I read that. *What about the four hundred and ninety-first time?* (Pause to do the math.) What Jesus was saying is that even after you lose count, keep forgiving.

The scripture 1 Corinthians 13 talks about love; in the midst of explaining what love is, the verse says, "Love keeps no record of wrong." After being wronged by the same person a few times, you probably won't want to put yourself in the same position with that particular person. We don't forgive others for their sake alone. We forgive them for our peace of mind. Remember how God forgives us over and over? The only way we can forgive deep hurt is through the help of the Lord.

So the Fifth Prayer Challenge is:

Lord, forgive me of my sins and help me to forgive others when they sin against me.

Taste and see that the Lord is good, blessed
is the one who takes refuge in Him.

—Psalm 34:8 (NIV)

CHAPTER 6

Our Daily Bread

In the Lord's Prayer, Jesus said, "Give us today our daily bread." It's short, but there is a lot there. What is our daily bread? The obvious answer is food. We have to eat every day to sustain life. If we don't eat every day, we starve and may get malnourished. As a child, did any of us starve or go without food for days? There are exceptions, but most of us can say no. Those needs were taken care of. Did we worry about the next day's meals? Again, most of us can say no. We had parents that took the responsibility of providing for us. I don't remember a time when I worried about that. As a matter of fact, when my mother called us for supper, I was always in a state of confidence and had a positive expectation of what delicious meal my mother had prepared that night. The only disappointing exception I can think of is when that liver she prepared looked like a juicy steak. Sorry for those of you who love liver, but the only thing good about liver and onions are…the onions. That disappointment happened only once that I can remember. I think it happened so that my siblings could tell that story (Jed's liver story) for the rest of my life. Even at my expense, I'm glad they have that fun story to tell over and over.

Our daily bread could also mean our needs for that day. How about a daily dose of God's word? In John 6:35 (NIV), Jesus declared, "I am the bread of life. Whoever comes to me will never go hungry and whoever believes in me will never go thirsty." Have you ever been hungry but you don't know what you're hungry for? You open up the refrigerator and search top to bottom but don't find anything that would fill the void in your stomach? People will do the same thing in life. They search for something to fill that void in their life but can't seem to find it. People often turn to things like alcohol, drugs, money, boyfriend, girlfriend, dog, or cat. Nothing seems to fill that void long-term. Jesus can fill that void. He can fill that empty and maybe anxious feeling that a person has in their life. Philippians 4:6–7(NIV) says,

> Do not be anxious about anything, but in every situation, by prayer and petition, with thanksgiving, present your requests to God. And the peace of God, which transcends all understanding, will guard your hearts and your minds in Christ Jesus.

We worry about a lot of things in life. Our daily needs, long term needs, and wants. If we lean on God's Word and promises, we can learn to live worry free. I don't want to come across as someone who never worried about things. I still worry about some of the things everybody else worries about. But the more I'm in God's Word, the more I can practice trusting in him. In Matthew 6:25–33 (NIV), Jesus says,

> Therefore I tell you, do not worry about your life, what you will eat or drink or your body, what you will wear. Is your life more than food and your body more than clothes? Look at the birds of the air, they do not sow or reap or store away in barns and yet your heavenly Father feeds them. Are you not much more valuable than they? Can any of you, by worrying, add a single hour to your life?

What Jesus is saying is, when we put our faith and trust in him and ask him for our daily needs (bread), he will be faithful and just to give us good gifts. Every good gift that we have comes from our Father in heaven, our provider. Some people would balk at that statement. They say, "Everything I have, I worked for myself!" Let's not be fooled. Everything we have, every talent we have is a blessing from God and he has a plan for our lives with the talents that he has given to each one of us. Some might say, "I don't need God! I'm doing okay without him." Then when things go wrong and they don't get what they want or can't control a situation, they might pray. But when God doesn't answer their prayers the way they want, they would say that God doesn't answer prayers or God doesn't care or God doesn't exist.

Every gift we desire is not necessarily a good gift in God's eyes. If a parent would give their children everything they want no matter what the cost and no matter what sacrifices they make, do you think that will bring that child closer to his or her parents? I have seen so many cases where it seems to do the opposite. I've seen a child grow up basically getting everything he asked for from his parents to the point that the parents were struggling financially trying to please him. When that child was in his twenties and had a job of his own, he was unable to afford the things he was accustomed to like 150-dollar tennis shoes, new matching furniture for his apartment, or a new car. He would then ask his parents to help out. The parents told him that they couldn't afford those things anymore, and he would have to buy less expensive tennis shoes or used furniture or a used car with over seventy thousand miles on it until he could afford to upgrade. I've heard stories that the child, in his twenties, would throw a fit because Mom and Dad wouldn't help out. The point is, buying affection only lasts until the next need or want arises. If you are looking at God like he is a genie, here to give us our three wishes a month, you might want to dig deeper into who God is and what he desires for us. It's okay to ask God for needs and wants that we have. He does want to bless us. Matthew 7:11 (NIV) says, "If you then, who are evil, know how to give good gifts to your children, how much more will your Father in heaven give good things to those who ask Him?" We have to examine the motives of the gifts we are asking for.

Some people don't ask for help from their parents or from God. I struggled a long time with asking God for things over the years. I would want some material thing, but I felt like it wouldn't be right to ask God for something like that. Why would God care about a trivial thing like that? But after reading several scriptures and listening to sermons, I realized that God cares about everything that we care about and wants to bless his children just as much as we would want to bless our children. So I began to ask God every time I desired something, mostly bigger items. If we involve God in big and small decisions, I believe we can limit the mistakes of buying ill-advised purchases we make.

I wanted a pole barn so I could have some place to put my mower, tools, a vehicle in, and a place to store things for the winter. Also, so I could put my car back in the garage. Is that kind of request going to change lives? No. It was just something that I desired to have to protect my necessary investments from the weather. So I prayed to God for that petition. I also added a request that I didn't want to go into debt for the barn. Would that be too difficult for God to answer? Nothing is too difficult for God! Did I have a plan in how God was going to accomplish this? Nope. I was just trying to practice a little faith. I tried for several months to find someone to build it. Everything seemed to fall through. I was getting a little frustrated, but God reminded me that his timing was worth waiting for rather than my timing. Finally, we found someone to give us a quote in person and not over the phone.

My wife, Michelle, and I felt good about this person, and I was kind of excited to see what kind of quote we were going to get. After all, this was God's timing, and we were confident that we were going to reap God's blessings. Then he came over with the quote. It was way more than I thought we could afford. I was discouraged. To give you a hint of what I'm like, I'm very tight with money that when I take a dollar bill from my wallet, the president squints. I don't like going into debt especially at fifty-eight years of age. The most discouraging part was that we had been praying about this for a long time, and I felt like we were back to square 1. Then Michelle says, "Wait a minute. What if we use this investment and move this money here?" After listening to her and talking about it further, I realized, *She was right!* (This will be Michelle's favorite part of the book.) We got the pole barn without going into debt. Sometimes, God uses people in our lives to help us out when we don't see the answer. We can't be too set in our ways to think that God is going to answer our prayers the way we think he should.

Now that long story may not have been a heartwarming story to read. It didn't heal a body or feed starving children, but what it did was show me how much God cares about every aspect of our lives, and if we put our trust in him, he will be faithful and just to answer our prayers. God does want to bless us. All we have to do is believe in him and trust that he will do what's best for us.

Have you ever been blessed by God without even asking for it? I work about an hour and a half from my house. It was a summer day, and I was headed home in the morning because I work the night shift. While I was traveling home, I was talking to Michelle. Relax. I have a Bluetooth, so I was hands free. We were just chatting about unimportant stuff. I said that I needed a new hat for mowing the lawn. One of those full rim hats, not a baseball cap style. My hair is white and short, and I burn easy. As I told her what kind of hat I wanted, I asked her where I could find a hat like that. The other hats I bought were bought on vacation at a souvenir shop. I didn't know of any hat stores around us. In the middle of our conversation, I told her I was going to stop at a gas station and I would call her back. I used the exit that I always use but stopped at a different gas station.

On my way to the restroom at that gas station, I passed a shelf. On that shelf was a hat. It caught my eye because it was the exact hat I was describing to Michelle. The hat looked out of place on that shelf because that was the only hat like it on that shelf. As a matter of fact, there were no other hats on that shelf, just bandanas and sunglasses and a few other items. I looked around, and there were no other hats in the store at all. I tried it on. It fit perfectly. I bought it. That blew my mind. I knew that was a gift from God! I didn't ask for it. I didn't even consider praying about it. It was such a trivial thing, but it was right on cue. In my mind, there was no other explanation for finding that hat at the particular moment. It was God telling me that he not only cares about the little things, he just wanted me to know that he listens to me and cares enough to show me that he desires to have a relationship with me. Every good gift doesn't have to be asked for. It's kind of like that feeling you get when your spouse, children, or parents give you a gift out of the blue. Meaning, it's not your birthday or Christmas. They just wanted to show you they were thinking about you and that they love you. That's the way I felt when God presented me with the hat.

Now, does God always give us what we ask for? No. Even if we are in God's Word everyday and pray often? Sometimes God says wait. Other times, God may say no. God has the advantage of knowing the future and what is good and bad for us. Some people think that if they win the lottery, all of their problems will go away. I could think of a lot of things that would cause hardship winning the lottery. Infidelity in the marriage, spending sprees to the point of losing everything, thieves targeting you to steal your wealth, etc. If you have all the money you need, then what? Would you have any more goals in your life? Do you think you will be truly happy? Famous actors and sports figures seem to have everything financially, but are they truly happy? Watch entertainment news or read the paper. A lot of them, not all of them, are miserable. Some have even taken their own life, and no one knows why. Some of them were loved dearly by fans and the media. So when God says no to a prayer, it's for a reason. A reason you may not see right away.

When Jesus was on earth, he had goals. His goal was to do his Father's will: save the lost, point them in the right direction, and show them how to live and think. Jesus was showing us what God was like and how he desires to have a relationship with us. Jesus was in constant prayer with God and knew God's plan for his life and how God wanted to accomplish it. Jesus would often go off by himself and pray. He must have been having the time of his life watching people getting saved and growing in their faith, but his time was getting short. In Matthew 26:39 (NIV), Jesus was in the Garden of Gethsemane praying. Overwhelmed with sorrow, he said, "My Father, if it is possible, may this cup be taken from me. Yet, not as I will, but as you will." Jesus knew the pain and suffering that was ahead of him on the cross and he was sorrowful and troubled as Matthew described.

If we knew what our future holds, especially a suffering that we would have to endure, I'm sure that we would have a lot of anxiety and sorrowful thoughts as well. But God did tell Jesus that there was no other way and that he would have to go through with the plan. This is good news for us because if he hadn't died on the cross and rose from the dead, there would be no redemption of sin. Now, God still loved Jesus very much and was still very much pleased with him. Jesus proved that there is nothing wrong with being honest with God and sharing your concerns and frightening moments with him. Even though God lets us go through some events in our life that's not pleasant, he will also give us courage to face those problems and that will make us stronger in our faith.

If we are in constant fellowship with the Lord, reading his Word and praying daily, he will turn even the most discouraging moments in our lives into a blessing. Simon Peter and his companions had been fishing all night. Summarizing Luke 5:1–11, they were cleaning their nets after a disappointing fishing trip. Actually, that was their career choice and how they made a living. Jesus walks up and climbs in Simon Peter's boat and asks him to push out farther in the water so he could preach to the crowd better. After he had finished, he told Peter to go into deeper water and let down his nets for a catch. Peter answered, "Master, we worked all night and caught nothing, but I will do as you say and let down the nets." When he did, they caught so many fish that he had to signal another boat to help bring the fish in. These men were professional fishermen. They knew the time of day to catch the most fish, and that wasn't the time, usually. Peter knew that was a miracle. The Lord took what Peter would call a bad day and turned it into something life-changing. Peter's life was changed that day forever just because he obeyed the Lord at that moment. When we don't obey God when he asks us to do something, what kind of blessings are we missing out? It could be life changing!

The Sixth and Final prayer challenge:

Lord, here are my petitions. I pray that they align with your will.

Taste and see that the Lord is good, blessed
is the one who takes refuge in Him.

—Psalm 34:8 (NIV)

EPILOGUE

Our Advocate

In the beginning of this book, I asked the question whether God is real or not and the ongoing debate of God versus science or evolution. So why do we, as Christians, debate this? Is it just to win the debate? What is our motive?

Christians believe in God most likely because we have had an experience in our hearts that confirms that God is real, and that, Jesus is the son of God that came to Earth to save us from our sins. So when a Christian says, 'God spoke to me," or "God is directing my path," we end up losing a lot of people. They usually think we have gone off the deep end. It seems like foolishness to someone who doesn't believe in God. We talk to people about this because we want other people to have the same experience with God as we do. The Bible clearly states that there are two places we go when we die: heaven with God, or hell (hades) where there is eternal torment.

There is a story in the Bible that Jesus tells that scares me every time I read it. Jesus told a lot of parables, and he often started them like, "There was a woman," or "There was a man with two sons." He never gave names to these characters in the stories. However, in Luke, he tells this story as if it really happened. He also names one of them. In Luke 16:19–31 (NIV),

> There was a rich man who was dressed in fine
> linen and lived in luxury every day. At the gate
> laid a beggar named Lazarus, covered with sores

and longing to eat what fell from the rich man's table. Even the dogs came and licked his sores. The time came when the beggar died, and the angels carried him to Abraham's side. The rich man also died and was buried. In hades, where he (the rich man) was in torment, he looked up and saw Abraham faraway and Lazarus by his side. So he called out to him, "Father Abraham, Have pity on me and send Lazarus to dip his finger in water and cool my tongue because I am in agony in this fire."

But Abraham replied, "Son, remember that in your lifetime you received good things while Lazarus received bad things. But now he is comforted and you are in agony. Besides all this, between us and you, a great chasm has been set in place so that those who want to go from here to you cannot, nor can anyone crossover from there to us."

Then he answered, "Then I beg you, Father, send Lazarus to my family, for I have five brothers. Let him warn them so that they will not also come to this place of torment.

Abraham replied, "They have Moses and the prophets. Let them listen to them."

"No Father Abraham," he said, "if someone from the dead goes to them, they will repent."

He said to him, "If they do not listen to Moses and the prophets, they will not be convinced even if someone rises from the dead.

After reading that story from the Bible, you can either choose to believe it or you can choose not to believe it. When I read that story, I put myself in Lazarus's place because I believe and put my trust in God. So you would think if I put myself in Lazarus's place, I would be happy and relieved. But as the rich man is in agony physically, I think I would be in agony in my heart for the one who was in torment, especially if I knew and loved that person when we were on earth together. That's the reason most Christians share their faith, because of love, not for the sake of being right.

There is really no way that I or any Christian can explain the peace that we have when we decided to believe in God and follow Jesus's example; that's why this book was written. In this world that we live in today, there are many opinions, and no one wants to take the word of someone else. So I'm not here to convince you either. I'm asking you to go off by yourself, and pray to God yourself. Speak to him as if he is standing there right beside you. Ask him like the first chapter says: "Lord if you're real, show me and speak to my heart." Now, if you say that with the right attitude and really seek God out, I believe you will have a blessed experience that you probably won't be able to explain to your friends. But don't just say it one time and wait for an answer. Say it every day, and show God that you really want to know the truth. It only takes about ten seconds of your day. But if you say it with the intensions of proving me, or other Christians wrong, don't bother. God won't speak to you with that attitude. God will not be mocked.

> The fear of the Lord is the beginning of knowledge, but fools despise wisdom and instruction. (Proverbs 1:7 NIV)

If you do have an experience and God speaks to your heart, and you wonder what to do next, it's very simple. All you have to do, to be saved and go to heaven after you die, is believe in God and acknowledge that Jesus is the Son of God and that he came to earth, died on the cross for our sins, and rose from the grave.

> For God so loved the world that he gave his one and only son that whoever believes in him shall not perish but have eternal life. (John 3:16 NIV)

A suggested prayer you can pray is this: "Dear God, I know I am a sinner, and I ask for your forgiveness. I believe that Jesus Christ is your son and that he died on the cross for my sins, and you raised him from the dead. I want to trust him as my savior and follow him from this day forward. Guide my life, and help me to do your will. Amen."

Once you have said that prayer or a prayer similar to that, you can consider yourself saved according to God's promise, and you will be in heaven with the Lord when you die. I would like to encourage you to talk to someone about your experience and get involved in a church somewhere that believes in the whole Bible as the Word of God.

If you are already saved and have accepted Jesus as your savior, are you serving God the way you want? Or are you just living your life, not reading or praying or only spending time with the Lord on Sundays? You are experiencing God's grace, but are you experiencing God's blessings? Have you ever been on a sports team, an academic team, or any kind of team for that matter? Were you content to just being on the team, sitting on the bench? Or did you want to play and contribute to the team? Has a coach ever said, "You're doing okay, but you are not where I like you to be." When the Lord grants salvation to you, he wants to help you grow in your faith. Notice I said "help you" grow in your faith.

Many of us try to help ourselves and not accept help from others or even God. God didn't plan for us to do it in that way. He doesn't want us to have to figure out life on our own. He knows that will be too difficult. Why not get help from the one who created life and everything in it. But how can God help us if we can't speak to him in person. In John 14:16–17 (NIV), Jesus is speaking,

> I will ask the Father, and he will give you another advocate to help you and be with you forever, the spirit of truth. The world cannot accept him because it neither sees him, nor knows him. But you know him for he lives with you and will be in you.

Jesus is talking about the Holy Spirit. The helper, advocate, that inner voice that we hear that tells us right from wrong; that inner voice that leads us to know how we are to act and how to encourage someone or lead us in the right direction.

> But the advocate, the Holy Spirit, when the Father will send in my name, will teach you all things and will remind you of everything that I have said to you. (John 14:26 NIV)

This means he will remind us what his word says and will give you answers to your problems. Father, Son, and Holy Spirit are the three in one. So when the Holy Spirit speaks to your heart, it's the same as God speaking to you.

If you want to hear from God and want to know what he wants for your life, the answer is simple: just ask him. Jesus gave us a prayer to pray that we call "the Lord's Prayer." Everything he said in that prayer is important for us to follow. I just expanded it, with the Lord's permission, of course, so I could share this as a six-step prayer challenge. Our daily bread, forgiveness, and forgiving others, leading us not into temptation. If you pray these things daily, God will speak to your heart and give you a new and exciting direction for your life… *Honest to God!*

> Taste and see that the Lord is good, blessed is the one who takes refuge in him.
>
> —Psalm 34:8 (NIV)

SIX-STEP PRAYER CHALLENGE

Step 1
God, if you are real, show me and speak to my heart.

Step 2
Lord, reveal yourself to me and give me a hunger for you
and your Word.

Step 3
Lord, change my direction, if necessary, so I can serve you the
way you want me to.

Step 4
Lord, help me to fight temptation and deliver me from
evil. Help me to put the full armor of God as in Ephesians.

Step 5
Lord, forgive me of my sins and help me to forgive others
when they sin against me.

Step 6
Lord, here are my petitions. I pray they align with
your will.

AUTHOR'S NOTE

My Testimony

I have gone to church all my life. I asked Jesus in my heart and got baptized at the age of eight. Like I said earlier, we never missed church, except when there was a snow emergency. I knew most of the stories in the Bible at a young age. I suppose I was like everyone else. I had dreams of what my future would hold. I experienced disappointments when those dreams would fall through. I wanted a good job, a wife, and children. I always desired to do what was right. I didn't like disappointing God, my parents, or anyone for that matter. Success is always the goal in everyone's life. I got a job in a factory. I liked hard labor at my young age. It was challenging, which I accepted. I got married and had two daughters. We went to church every Sunday morning, Sunday night, and Wednesday night. God was still important in my life but wasn't a priority, I'm sorry to say. I got caught up in my work, family, and the activities in our lives. Time spent with God suffered. I was just too busy. I would say, "When things settle down, I'll have more time to spend with God." Well, time went by, my marriage dissolved, my job closed and went overseas, so I went back to school to get another career. My daughters were in junior high and high school. Now we were looking into college for the girls.

After I graduated, I started working. I picked up extra shifts because I felt I was behind financially. I met Michelle at one of the hospitals I worked at. We got married. She has two daughters as well. I am very proud of all four of our daughters. At this time in my life,

I thought things were supposed to slow down so I can spend more time with God. Maybe if I work hard and retire early, I can spend more time with God then. That's okay, you can call me foolish.

I was in my fifty's; I'm ashamed to say when I got frustrated and realized that I can't serve the Lord the way I want to without his help. So in my frustration, I said, "God, reveal yourself to me and give me a hunger for you and your Word." It took me getting humble before God and admitting I couldn't serve him by my own power to start that change in my life. That honest moment changed my spiritual life for the better. My mind was renewed. He started opening up scriptures to me. He increased my faith. He started speaking to me and leading me in areas that I never dreamed. I am learning more and more everyday from God. All I had to do was to realize my absolute need of him.

I also asked God to help me see people the way he sees people. Therefore, he had given me more understanding and compassion for people. With that new compassion for people, I want every one of my family and friends to know the God that I know and to accept Jesus as their savior.

Living a Christian life is sometimes hard especially without Christ in the center of your life. Matthew 19:26 (NIV) says, "With man this is impossible, but with God, all things are possible." I never claimed to be a smart person. I struggled in school. I didn't standout or do anything spectacular. I didn't break any records in sports or academics. I don't have all the answers, but I do know where to go to get answers. Now when I have a problem, big or small, I seek God for the right path to take rather than rely on my own wisdom.

When I depend on God and spend time with him daily, He speaks to me and asks me to do things I thought I would never do. Writing this book is one of those things. When I felt like God wanted me to write a book, the first thing I did was laugh. It reminded me of the story from the Old Testament when God gave Abraham and Sarah a son when Sarah was ninety years old. In Genesis 21:6 (NIV), Sarah said, "God has brought me laughter and everyone who hears about this will laugh with me."

I imagine my high school English teacher will be one of those who will laugh the loudest. The second thing I thought was there is no way I can do this. I don't have what it takes to write a book. Then God reminded me that Moses had the same concerns when God told him to lead the children of Israel out from bondage in Egypt. Now, by no means am I comparing myself to Moses, but when God is leading you to do something, and he guides you every step of the way, you have no choice but to give God all the credit.

> Trust in the Lord with all your heart and lean not on your own understanding, in all your ways, submit to Him, and He will make your paths straight. (Proverbs 3:5–6 NIV)

I listen to podcasts of a well-known pastor in Georgia. I have adopted one of his favorite sayings and applied it to my life. It goes like this: "Obey God and leave all the consequences to him."

I believe this prayer challenge can change lives. These six-prayer challenges are merely suggestions on what to pray for. You can certainly change them to fit your needs. Just being honest with God is a start. I have new and exciting expectations of what God wants me to do next in my life. My prayer is that God has encouraged you in some way. May God bless you and your family for generations to come.

ABOUT THE AUTHOR

Jed Morehouse grew up in Brookston, Indiana. He entered the workforce following graduation from high school. He worked in a factory for twenty years before the factory shut down operations and moved to China and Mexico. He then went to college to become a respiratory therapist and has worked in a hospital setting for the last sixteen years. After putting God at the center of his life, he wanted to share what God has revealed to him. *Honest to God* is his first book.

www.ingramcontent.com/pod-product-compliance
Lightning Source LLC
Chambersburg PA
CBHW021143130726
47988CB00003B/1437